Piano Vocal Guitar

MW01553806

™ Rhino Ent. Co.

Photography by Gene Trindl

ISBN 0-7935-9343-3

7777 W. BLUEMOUND RD. P.O. BOX 13819 MILWAUKEE, WI 53213

For all works contained herein:
Unauthorized copying, arranging, adapting, recording or public performance is an infringement of copyright.
Infringers are liable under the law.

Visit Hal Leonard Online at
www.halleonard.com

CONTENTS

Page	Title
9	Daydream Believer
12	D.W. Washburn
16	The Girl I Knew Somewhere
21	Goin' Down
30	Heart and Soul
36	I Wanna Be Free
42	I'm a Believer
39	It's Nice to Be with You
46	Last Train to Clarksville
52	Listen to the Band
49	A Little Bit Me, A Little Bit You
56	Mary, Mary
66	Theme from "The Monkees" (Hey, Hey We're the Monkees)
59	Pleasant Valley Sunday
70	The Porpoise Song
74	Randy Scouse Git
80	(I'm Not Your) Steppin' Stone
83	That Was Then, This Is Now
88	Valleri
92	Words

Still Monkees After All These Years
by Mark Etzkorn

*Anytime or anywhere
Just look over your shoulder
Guess who'll be standin' there*

—from "Hey, Hey, We're The Monkees"

They might not have been John, Paul, George and Ringo, but Mike (Nesmith), Micky (Dolenz), Davy (Jones) and Peter (Tork) — a.k.a. the Monkees — are indeed still standing, taller than ever. While most of their contemporaries have long since been designated to the pop-culture trash heap, the Monkees have managed to carve out an enduring niche for themselves in the musical history books — all the more impressive since their career really only lasted about two years.

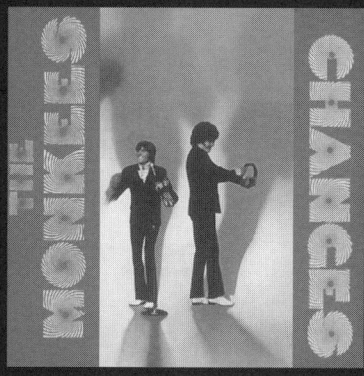

But oh, what a two years it was. "Last Train to Clarksville," "Daydream Believer," "Mary, Mary," "(I'm Not Your) Steppin' Stone," "Valleri," "Pleasant Valley Sunday," "I'm a Believer"— you know them, you love them. And now, a generation after the Monkees first hit the TV and radio airwaves, it's cooler than ever to confess that affection.

That wasn't always the case. Although they were a fabulous commercial success during their brief heyday (late 1966 to 1969), the Monkees were the Rodney Dangerfields of the mid- to late-60s pop scene, getting no respect from "serious" music fans who perceived them as little more than a Beatles rip-off.

Which they were — initially. Conceived from the start by TV executives (and musical impresario Don Kirshner) to capitalize on the phenomenal success of the lads from Liverpool, the Monkees were a TV show first and a band second (only two of the members, Nesmith and Tork, had any previous musical experience). They only sang— not played— on their first two albums, a secret that when it escaped led to such smirking labels as the "Pre-Fab Four."

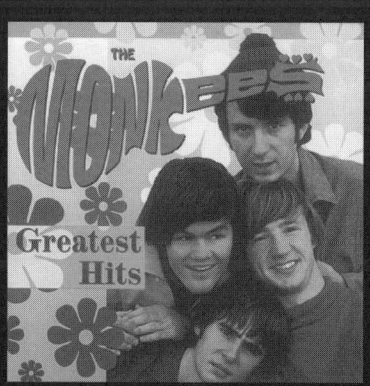

What their critics overlooked was that with the help of some of the best songwriters of the era — Tommy Boyce and Bobby Hart, Gerry Goffin and Carole King, Jerry Leiber and Mike Stoller, Neil Diamond, and Neil Sedaka — the Monkees produced some tremendously entertaining and enduring pop records. Light as a feather? Maybe. Well-crafted, expertly executed, and exuberant? Undoubtedly. They also were thankfully free of the sociopolitical self-seriousness that makes so many songs of the era almost impossible to listen to today. Even when they tried to engage in a little spirit-of-the-times social commentary, such as in "Pleasant Valley Sunday," it still came out sounding like they were too busy singin' to put anybody down.

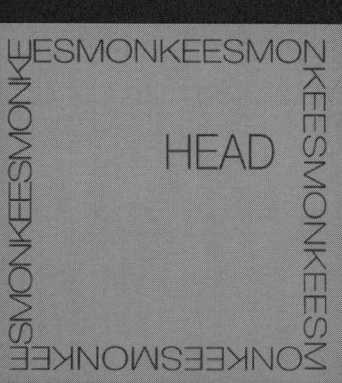

Made for TV

The individual Monkees had never met before they were plucked from anonymity to star in a new TV show. They were a diverse crew. Dolenz was a show biz kid who had worked as a child actor on TV. Jones was a horse jockey and sometime stage actor and singer in England. Tork had relocated to California after working the Greenwich Village folk circuit. Nesmith, a Texan into country music, had played in a few bands and done a little recording in L.A..

The show's producers, intent on reproducing the energy and irreverence of the Beatles classic film *A Hard Day's Night*, threw the charismatic unknowns together and dubbed them The Monkees. It was the perfect marketing vehicle. There was a guy for every 16-year-old girl to fall in love with: Davy, the cute one; Micky, the zany one; Peter, the shy, a-little-on-the-slow-side one, and Mike, the talented, laid-back, slightly-more-responsible one. And on top of all that, the music was undeniably catchy.

The Monkees debuted on NBC in September 1966, featuring the escapades of the fun-loving musicians as they experienced the Swinging '60s, grooving in their cool '60s pad, falling in love with cool '60s chicks, and dishing up a few cool songs every week. The show was an immediate hit, and a string of Monkee singles (starting with "Last Train to Clarksville," which actually was released early to pave the way for the show's debut) and albums quickly shot up the charts. The monstrous success demanded a tour, of course, and the non-musician members, Dolenz and Jones, had to quickly develop their musical chops. They were able to pull it off satisfactorily, even if Jones pretty much stuck to the tambourine.

Behind the scenes

The music for the Monkees' early albums was recorded by an all-star roster of L.A. studio musicians — the Monkees only sang. The TV honchos and musical producers were incredibly hesitant to let the band's secret (that they weren't really a band) get out, or risk the phenomenal sales of the early releases by giving the group any creative control.

Nesmith spearheaded a drive to get the Monkees to be able to perform as well as sing on their records. It wasn't easy, but when he finally succeeded it was apparent the executive's fears were unfounded. The new records sold just as much as the old ones. Nesmith was himself a talented songwriter, contributing hits like "Mary, Mary," "The Girl I Knew Somewhere," and "Listen to the Band." (He also wrote Linda Ronstadt's first hit, "Different Drummer," which she recorded in 1968 with her band the Stone Poneys.)

The Monkees' music was surprisingly eclectic and inventive, spanning their trademark pop ("Clarksville," "I'm a Believer," "Valleri"), pseudo-psychedelia ("Words"), garage band grunge ("Steppin' Stone"— c'mon, it was grungy for the Monkees), sigh-inducing ballads ("I Wanna Be Free") and whimsical anomalies ("D.W. Washburn").

In less than three years, the Monkees racked up 11 Top-40 hits and managed to sell 16 million albums and more than seven million singles. In 1967, the year of the Beatles' summer-of-love opus *Sgt. Pepper's Lonely Hearts Club Band*, the top-selling album was the Monkees' second effort, *More of the Monkees*. The band also captured the number three and number seven spots that year with their third and fourth releases, *Headquarters*, and *Pisces, Aquarius, Capricorn & Jones Ltd*. Their first four albums all went to number one on the charts, and for a while at least, Monkeemania eclipsed Beatlemania.

Monkees just want to have fun

The trivia surrounding the Monkees is almost as fun as the band itself. Nesmith's mother was a former secretary who made a fortune by inventing Liquid Paper. Actors and musicians turned down at the show's casting call included Paul Williams, Danny Hutton (soon to be of Three Dog Night), and Stephen Stills (Crosby, Stills, Nash and Young).

Musicians who played on Monkees records included Harry Nilsson, Leon Russell, Jack Nitzsche, Ry Cooder, Neil Young, Stephen Stills (again), Buddy Miles, and Glenn Campbell. The Monkees' 1968 movie, *Head*, a kind of surreal extension of the TV show, was co-written by Jack Nicholson and featured appearances by Frank Zappa, Annette Funicello, Victor Mature, and Terri Garr. (The film flopped at the box office but remains a cult favorite. Apparently, people wanted their Monkees wacky, but not *weird*.)

The Monkees also helped introduce Jimi Hendrix to American audiences after Dolenz saw the groundbreaking guitarist performing in London in 1967 and invited him to open for the band on the remainder of their U.S. tour that year. Unfortunately, after two weeks of hostile reactions from hordes of shell-shocked teenage girls, Hendrix quit in frustration.

The end for the Monkees came all too soon. NBC canceled the show in 1968 and Tork threw in the towel shortly thereafter (the others continued to record for another year or so). The band members struck out on their own paths, with Nesmith probably enjoying the most interesting career. He went on to pursue an increasingly ambitious musical career with the First National Band before finding his way into video and film production (including the cult classic *Repo Man*).

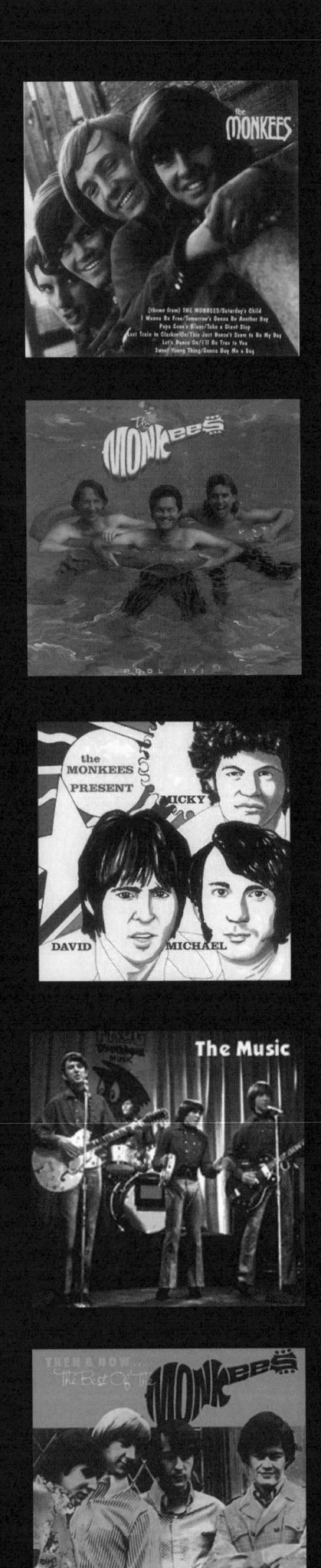

Monkees forever

The band enjoyed a surge of renewed popularity in the mid- to late-1980s when MTV began re-airing the old TV shows and their music began creeping back onto the charts. The band, *sans* Nesmith, re-assembled, embarked on a tour (Mike eventually joined them for a few dates), recorded a few new songs (including "That Was Then, This Is Now"), and got a star on the Hollywood Walk of Fame. One downside to the revival was that it spawned the abysmal *The New Monkees*, an uninspired and uninspiring update of the original TV show.

In the mid-90s Rhino Records released "Justus,"the first CD of new music by the complete, original Monkees in nearly 30 years. Another successful tour soon followed. Rhino, who acquired the rights to the Monkees' entire catalogue, started re-releasing all the old albums (as well as previously unheard material), and Monkees retrospectives and documentaries started popping up all over the TV dial. Monkee websites flourished.

It may have taken 30 years, but the world has finally learned to appreciate the Monkees for what they were — the source of some of the most enjoyable and inventive American pop music of the '60s. Come and watch them sing and play.

DAYDREAM BELIEVER

Words and Music by
JOHN STEWART

© 1967 (Renewed 1995) SCREEN GEMS-EMI MUSIC INC.
All Rights Reserved   International Copyright Secured   Used by Permission

Additional Lyrics

VAMP 1
Goin' down, goin' down, goin' down, goin' down,
Goin' down, goin' down, goin' down, goin' down.
I wish I'd look before I leap;
I didn't know it was so deep.
Been down so far I don't get wet.
I haven't touched the bottom yet.

VAMP 2
This river scene is getting old.
I'm hungry, sleepy, wet and cold.
She told me to forget it nice;
I should have taken her advice.
I only wanna go on home.
I'd gladly leave that girl alone.
What a way to spend the night;
If I don't drown I'll die of fright.
My pappy taught me how to float,
But I can't swim a single note.
He threw me in to teach me how;
I stayed there floatin' like a mama cow
And now I've floated way downstream.
I know this has to be a dream.

VAMP 3
If I could find my way to shore
I'd never never do this any more.
They give you three, I've been down nine,
I'm a'-goin' down just one more time.

VAMP 4
Goin' down, goin' down, goin' down, goin' down,
I'm goin' down, goin' down, back, back, back, back home,
Back, back, back, home. Back,
Back, back, back home.
Goin' down, goin' down,
I'm goin' down.
I'm goin' back home.

VAMP 5

Back to my friends,
Back to the one.
Back to do with the truth.
I'm goin' home.

VAMP 6

(Tacet)

VAMP 7
Now the sky is getting light, and
Ev'rything will be all right.
Think I've finally got the nack of just
Floatin' and lazin' on my back.
I never really liked that town.
I think I'll ride the river down,
Just moving slow and a'floating free.
This a river swinging under me
Waving back to the suckers on shore.
I should have thought of this before.

VAMP 8
I'll float on down to New Orleans
And pick up on some swingin' scenes.
I'm gonna know a better day.
I'll go down groovin' all the way.
I'm goin' down.

IT'S NICE TO BE WITH YOU

Words and Music by
JERRY GOLDSTEIN

Copyright © 1968 Jerry Goldstein Music, Inc.
Copyright Renewed
All Rights Administered by Songs Of PolyGram International, Inc.
International Copyright Secured All Rights Reserved

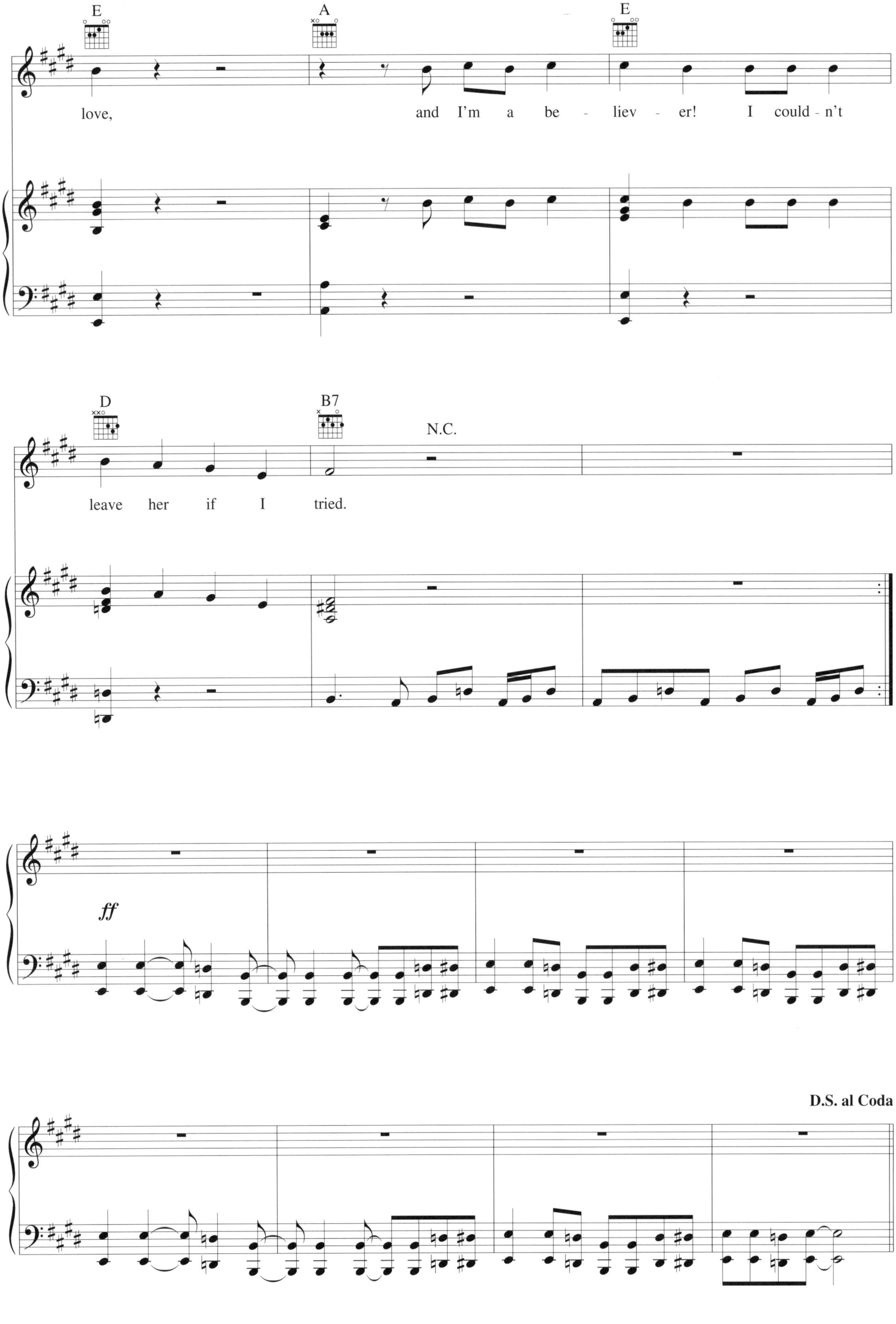

love, and I'm a be-liev-er! I could-n't leave her if I tried.

D.S. al Coda

Last Train to Clarksville

Words and Music by BOBBY HART and TOMMY BOYCE

© 1966 (Renewed 1994) SCREEN GEMS-EMI MUSIC INC.
All Rights Reserved   International Copyright Secured   Used by Permission

50

PLEASANT VALLEY SUNDAY

Words and Music by GERRY GOFFIN
and CAROLE KING

THEME FROM "THE MONKEES"
(Hey, Hey We're The Monkees)

Words and Music by TOMMY BOYCE
and BOBBY HART

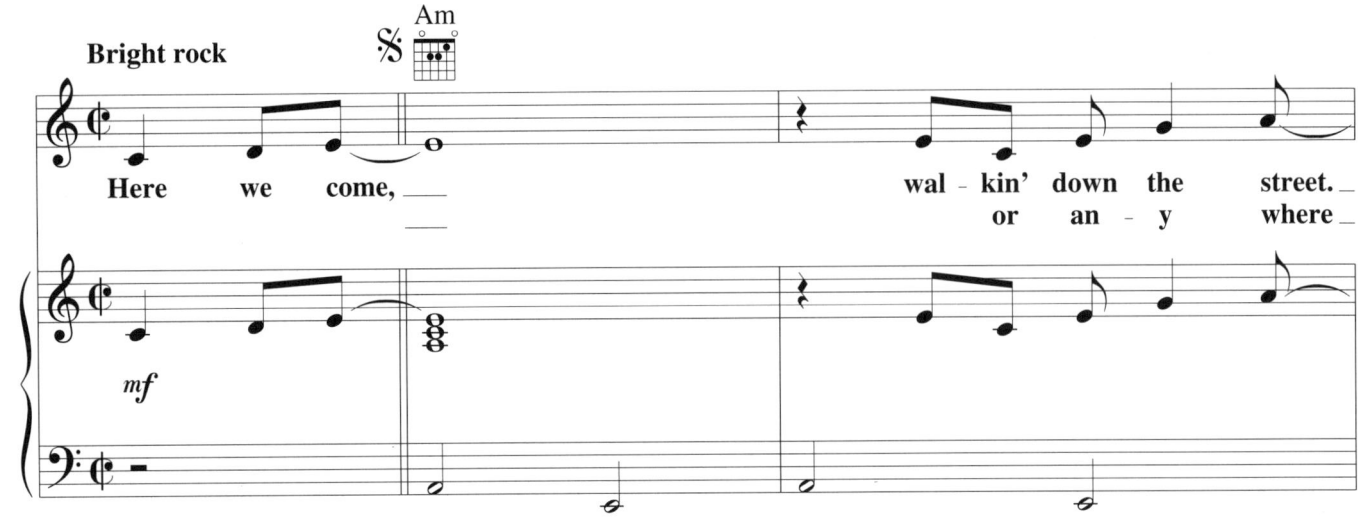

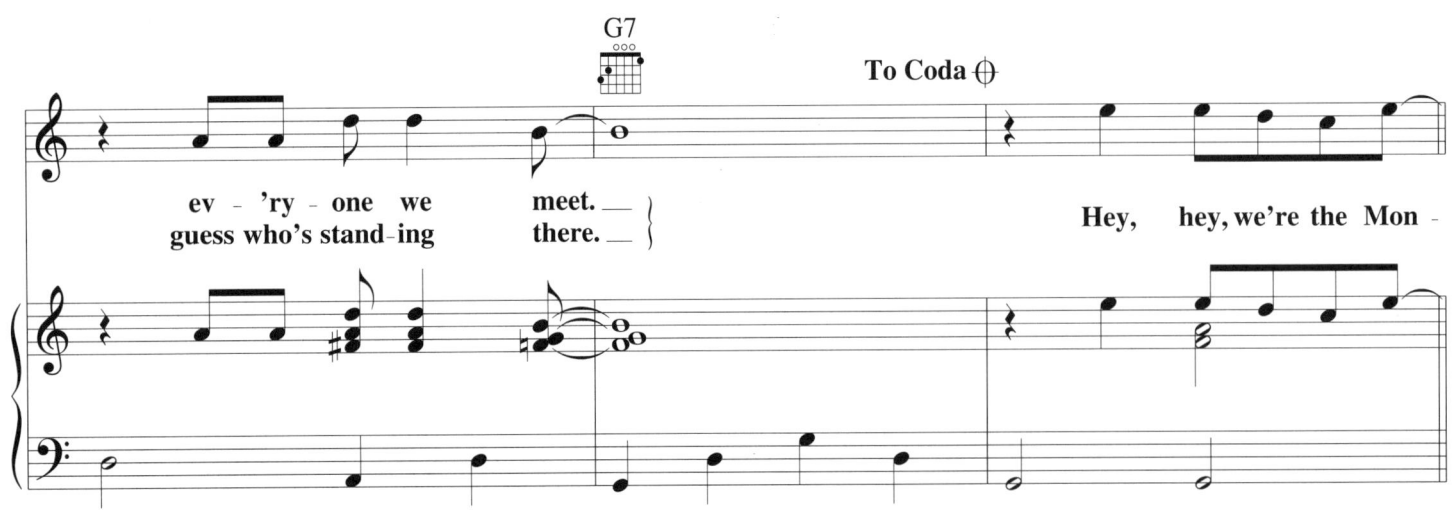

© 1966 (Renewed 1994) SCREEN GEMS-EMI MUSIC INC.
All Rights Reserved   International Copyright Secured   Used by Permission

(I'm Not Your) Steppin' Stone

Words and Music by TOMMY BOYCE and BOBBY HART

Moderately

I, I, I, I, I'm not your step-ping stone.
I, I, I, I, I'm not your step-ping stone.

You're try-ing to make your mark in so-ci-ety
I first met you, girl, you did-n't have no shoes,

us-ing all the tricks that you used on me. You're
but now you're walk-in' 'round like you're front page news.

© 1966 (Renewed 1994) SCREEN GEMS-EMI MUSIC INC.
All Rights Reserved   International Copyright Secured   Used by Permission

THAT WAS THEN, THIS IS NOW

Words and Music by
VANCE BRESCIA

VALLERI

Words and Music by BOBBY HART and TOMMY BOYCE

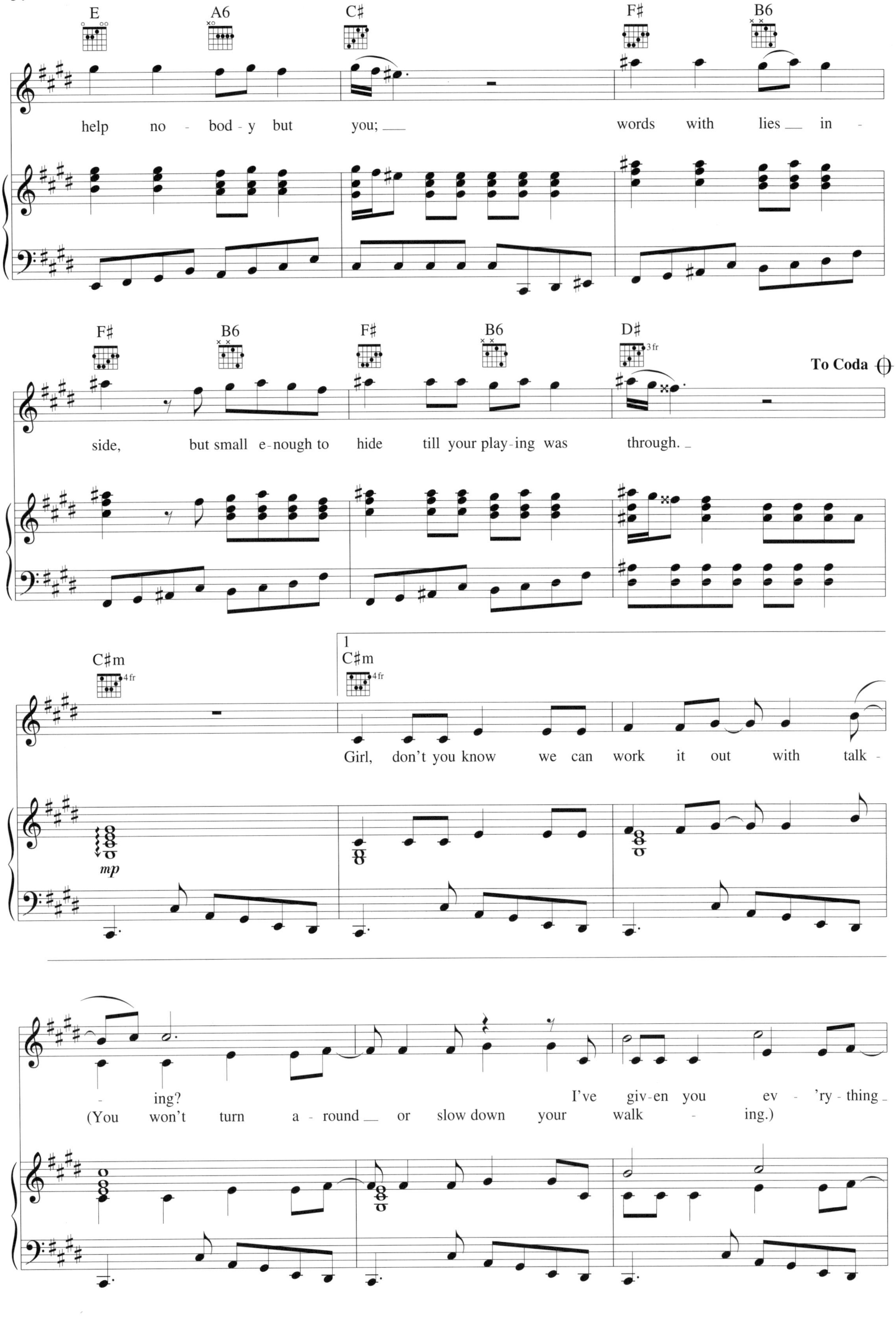
E A6 C♯ F♯ B6
help no - bod - y but you;
words with lies in -
F♯ B6 F♯ B6 D♯
side, but small e - nough to hide till your play - ing was through.
To Coda
C♯m
mp
1
C♯m
Girl, don't you know we can work it out with talk -
- ing?
(You won't turn a - round or slow down your walk - ing.)
I've giv - en you ev - 'ry - thing